EVERYDAY
MADE EASY

SIBELIUS
MUSIC APP
BASICS

Publisher and Creative Director: Nick Wells
Commisioning Editor: Polly Prior
Senior Project Editor: Catherine Taylor
Art Director & Layout: Mike Spender
Digital Design and Production: Chris Herbert
Copy Editor: Anna Groves
Screenshots: Andy Bell

Special thanks to: Taylor Bentley, Dawn Laker, Eileen Cox

This edition first published 2019 by
FLAME TREE PUBLISHING
6 Melbray Mews
Fulham, London SW6 3NS
United Kingdom

www.flametreepublishing.com

© 2019 Flame Tree Publishing

19 21 23 22 20
1 3 5 7 9 10 8 6 4 2

ISBN 978-1-78755-299-9

A CIP record for this book is available from the British Library upon request.

Printed in China

Everyday Guides Made Easy: Sibelius Music App Basics is an independent publication and has not been
authorized, sponsored, or otherwise approved by Avid Technology, Inc. and related product names are
trademarks of Avid Technology, Inc..

Image Credits:
Screenshots courtesy of Andy Bell.
Product shots courtesy of and ©: **Avid Technology, Inc.** 7, 11; **M-Audio**: 32
All remaining photos courtesy **Shutterstock.com** and © the following contributors: Africa Studio: 41, 55, 58, 115;
Sandra R. Barba: 94; Aleksey Boyko: 102; antb: 3; argus: 12; ASB63: 1; dean bertoncelj: 51; Billion Photos: 92; DavidSamperio:
front cover (top), 96; Dmytro Vietrov: 72; ESB Professional: 82; FlashMovie: 118; Aleksandar Grozdanovski: 89; ignai: 10;
Labutin.Art: 87; LucVi: 52; Luminis: 33; Oleksiy Mark: front cover (bottom), 109; Masyanya: 51; Wiktoria Matynia: 13;
MintImages: 22, 40; NatalyLad: 34; Negnut: 39; Vlad Andrei Nica: 42; NicoElNino: 111; Pixel-Shot: 45, 83, 120; Pop-Tika: 8;
PrinceOfLove: 5, 44, 99; Rachaphak: 57; rarrarorro: 80; Redshinestudio: 76; Trum Ronnarong: 121; Stokkete: 6, 105; TAK L: 90;
Triff: 84; UfaBizPhoto : 97; Vectorry: 79; VladKK: 106; Wikicommons: 21; lena Yakobchuk: 24, 30

EVERYDAY GUIDES
MADE EASY

SIBELIUS
MUSIC APP
BASICS

ANDY BELL

FOREWORD BY RONAN MACDONALD

FLAME TREE
PUBLISHING

CONTENTS

Getting familiar with the application and starting a new document.

An introduction to the different ways of entering notes, percussion symbols
and guitar tablature into your score.

A guide to adding notation symbols to your music: lyrics, expressions,
articulations, dynamics, slurs and other shapes.

How to move, copy, delete, correct and adjust parts of your score,
as well as lay out the music on to pages.

A guide to all the things you can do with your score when it's complete:
exporting to other formats and working with audio playback.

An introduction to the powerful capabilities of Sibelius: tools
for fine adjustments, plugins for special tasks.

FOREWORD

Considered by many composers the ultimate music notation toolbox, Sibelius goes far, far beyond the limitations of pen and paper. It gives you everything you need to create, share, print and listen to professional-quality scores on your Mac or PC.

From the initial capture of musical ideas via MIDI input or mouse, through the editing and refining of notes, markings and aesthetic elements into a beautiful finished score, all the way to mixing and rendering a polished performance of your composition using an enormous on-board library of sampled virtual instruments, Avid's amazing package is geared up to handle every stage of the process.

With great power, however, comes a certain degree of complexity. Although Sibelius is admirably intuitive in its interface and workflow, it's still a very high-end application with a considerable learning curve – which is where this eBook comes in. A comprehensive guide to Sibelius, *Sibelius Made Easy* takes you through all of the software's core concepts and features – as well as many of its deeper, more advanced systems – presenting them in a jargon-free, easy-to-follow way. Whether you're a total beginner in search of the quickest possible route to Sibelius mastery, or an experienced user looking to brush up on the basics, you've come to the right place.

Ronan Macdonald
Music technology writer and editor

INTRODUCTION

Sibelius is a professional music notation app made by Sibelius Software Limited, now part of Avid Technology. It combines features found in word processors and graphics and audio workstations to make it easy to create a musical manuscript and prepare it for dissemination.

STARTING SIBELIUS

Sibelius has the power to produce notation to suit any genre of music. This might leave the musician feeling a little overwhelmed, unsure of where to start, and how best to use Sibelius to get the most out of their score. However, the user is presented with a huge variety of tools to aid them in their musical creation, all of which may be useful at some point.

This book is aimed at guiding you through the process of creating notation in Sibelius. It will track the process through the creation of the manuscript to sharing its parts with others, detailing how to enter notes, articulations, and outlining the best practices of presentation.

SIBELIUS VERSIONS

Sibelius works almost identically on both Windows and Mac operating systems, although there are differences in keyboard shortcuts between them. Shortcuts will be presented as Key + Letter. Command will act as equivalent to Ctrl on a Windows keyboard; any outliers will be stated.

Above: This could be a result of your score preparation with Sibelius.

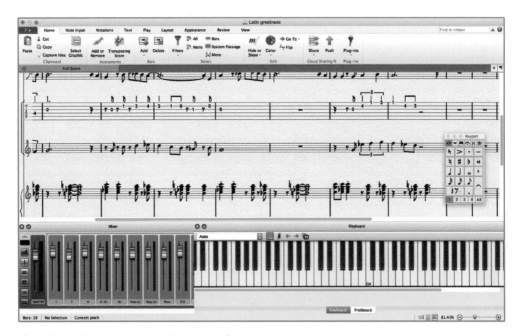

Above: Sibelius will help turn your musical ideas into a professional-looking score.

There are three different versions of Sibelius you can choose from, depending on what's necessary for your workflow. Sibelius First is free, but comes with its own set of limitations. However, it's ideal for beginners and is sufficient for their needs.

The other versions can be purchased either through subscription or a perpetual licence, as is standard with Avid products. This book will accommodate Sibelius First users, but will also incorporate explanations and advice that are only available in paid versions of the software.

Hot Tips

Whether you're a complete novice or a seasoned professional, there will be something in this eBook for everyone. Hot Tips will provide information on how to speed up your workflow and make Sibelius work better for you.

GETTING STARTED

STARTING YOUR SCORE

Sibelius is available as a download. This consists of the program, its constituent sounds and the Avid Application Manager. To install, work through these systematically. Once that's done, you're ready to start your score music!

AUTHORIZATION

Once you've installed your copy of Sibelius and opened the software for the first time, you'll be asked to authorize your account. You will be prompted on whether to continue your trial, activate your account, or open Sibelius First. If you choose to activate, you will be given a series of boxes to complete.

Below: Get ready to write!

Above: Follow the instructions in order to activate your account.

FONTS

There's a variety of fonts that come with the Sibelius software. You can use these in other programs too.

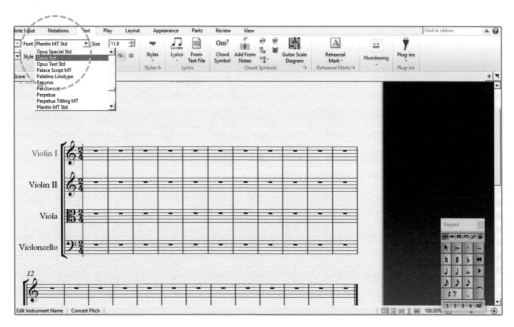

Above: Give your score a different feel with any of the number of fonts provided by Sibelius. You can install your own too.

TERMINOLOGY

It's necessary to understand some ubiquitous musical terminology to get the most out of Sibelius.

STAFF

The staff is the five lines on which music is notated. The plural is staves.

Above: The staff, or stave is the set of lines on which musical notes are written.

SYSTEM

A group of connected staves; there are usually two or three systems to a page, depending on size.

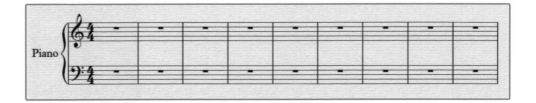

Above: Systems lock groups of instruments together. Notes aligned vertically indicate that they are played at the same time as each other.

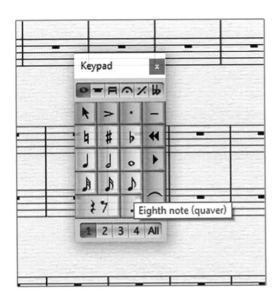

US vs UK ENGLISH

Sibelius allows for the use of both UK and US English musical terms and does not take preference over which is shown, generally providing both when necessary.

Left: You can always be sure you're using the software correctly, as Sibelius gives both UK and US English options.

Should you wish to use Sibelius in any other languages, there are multiple languages available to choose from in the Sibelius Preferences bar. There are also workflow preferences to do with how the mouse moves, shortcuts and more, as well as changing skins and overall aesthetic features of the software.

Right: The Preference tab includes options to customize Sibelius to work exactly how you'd like.

QUICK START

Quick Start is the command centre of Sibelius. You'll see this window every time you launch Sibelius or close a score.

① LEARN

Watch tutorials, open the manual and compare reference scores, of which there are multiple styles showcasing what Sibelius can offer. This includes a Vocal score, Funk, Jazz and an Orchestral Score.

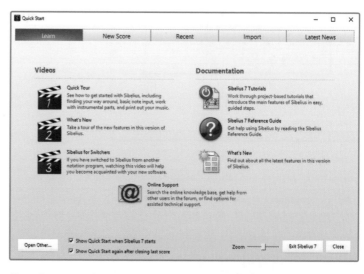

Above: Get to grips with creating a score in Sibelius with the Learn tab from the Quick Start guide.

② NEW SCORE

Create a new work from multiple templates, ranging from a single treble clef to mariachi bands to symphony orchestras. You can also create a blank score, enabling you to work totally from scratch and dictate the instruments for which you are writing. You can click on the template to see what's included.

Templates are a great starting point if you want to work quickly, or to generate ideas.

Learn New Score Recent Import Latest News

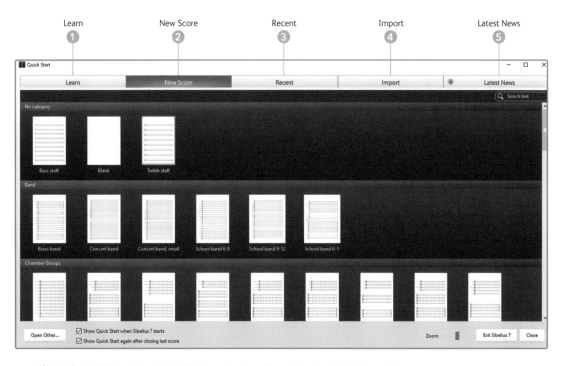

Above: The Quick Start window, showing the Learn, New Score, Recent, Import and Latest News options.

❸ RECENT

Scores that you've worked on in the last month will be shown here. You can see the fine details of a project to ensure you're opening the exact copy you need.

Title: II. Anonymous
Subtitle: Villanella (end of 16th c.)
Pages: 9, **Duration:** 3:35
Filename: C:\Users\Admin\Documents\Scores\Backup Scores\Ancient Dances and Airs - String Parts - mvt II_52.sib

Above: Sibelius will show you the necessary information to ensure you open the correct project.

Open Other...

Open scores that aren't available under Recent by clicking here.

❹ IMPORT

Here you can convert and import MIDI information that has been exported from elsewhere. You can dictate how Sibelius will receive and translate the MIDI into score.

MusicXML Files

As well as MIDI, you can also import MusicXML files, allowing you to open projects that have been created in other notation software.

Hot Tip

Should you wish to close Sibelius at this point, just press Exit on the Quick Start window.

Above: You can open scores made in other software here, if it has been exported as MusicXML. Some versions of Sibelius also offer the ability to transcribe or scan other scores and convert to Sibelius notation.

❺ LATEST NEWS

The final section of the Quick Start menu shows you the latest news regarding Avid, their products and updates to Sibelius.

SETTING UP YOUR SCORE

Setting up your score is incredibly simple in Sibelius. You have all the building blocks to create a professional, easy-to-read score.

TEMPLATES

From the Quick Start menu, choose New and you will see a series of templates of scores of different types, as can be seen in the image below.

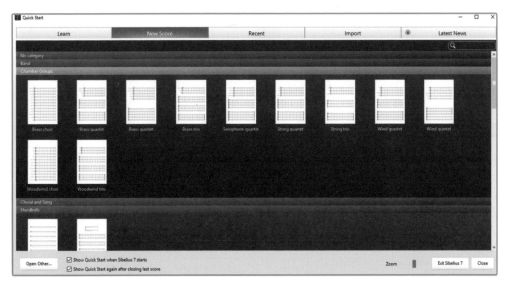

Above: The New Score dialog box.

DOCUMENT SETUP

The default page size for a Sibelius score is A4, but should you already know the size to which you are printing, specify it here. Other options include concert scores, hymn books and more, which can be seen below. When adding instruments after the score has been set up, Sibelius will always give you the option to change your score size in order to make sure everything fits.

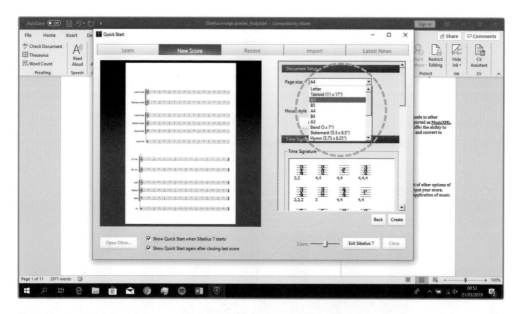

Above: There are a whole host of page size options to choose from, allowing you to create scores for any type of music.

House Style

This dictates the overall look of the score. You can change it from a multitude of printed typefaces to handwritten styles, as might be found on jazz lead sheets.

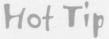

Hot Tip

Change the size of the paper later in the process by using the shortcut Command + D.

Change Instruments

Find the instruments to include in your score here and Sibelius will arrange them conventionally on your page. Type what you are looking for in the Find bar or use drop-down menus that arrange the vast collection of available instruments into their traditional families.

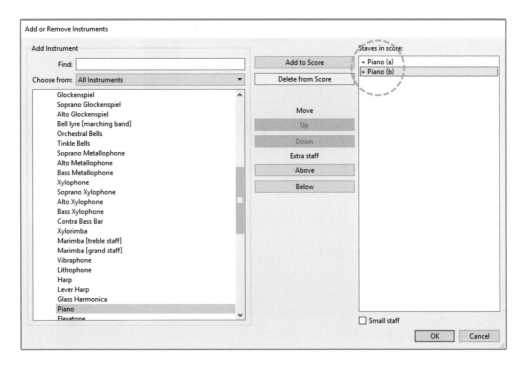

Above: Here, Piano (b) is deleted.

For grand-staved instruments (the piano or marimba, for example), you might only intend to make use of one stave. After the instrument has been added, select the half you'd like to remove – the right hand is 'Piano (a)' and left is 'Piano (b)' – and press Delete from Score to remove it. This is helpful for saving space in a busy score.

Hot Tip

You can double-click the name of the instrument to add it instead of moving the mouse to Add to Score. This can also be used when deleting instruments from the score.

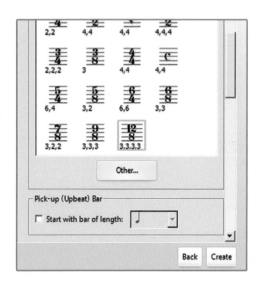

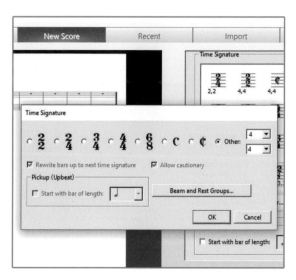

Above: Follow these steps to create a custom time signature.

Time Signature Setup

Add an instrument before setting the time signature of your score. You can choose from the most commonly used time signatures, or add your own by clicking Other > Other and typing or selecting the time signature, as shown in the screenshots above.

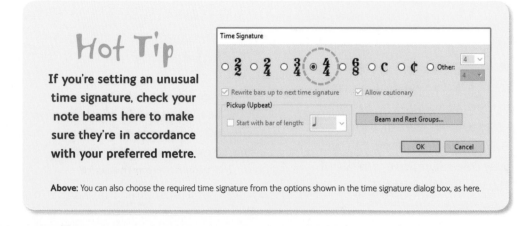

Hot Tip

If you're setting an unusual time signature, check your note beams here to make sure they're in accordance with your preferred metre.

Above: You can also choose the required time signature from the options shown in the time signature dialog box, as here.

Pick-up (Upbeat) Bar

If your piece starts with an upbeat, select it here to save any future hassle of adding weirdly timed bars. Note that deleting a bar that includes an upbeat – the beat before the first beat of a measure – will also cause the title and composer's credits of your score to be deleted..

Above: If you know your score starts with an upbeat, add it when you create your score; you can select the duration of the note with which it starts from an easy-to-use dropdown menu.

Tempo

You can add the Italian, French, German or English tempo markings via the drop-down menu or by typing it in. It is a good idea to leave this blank and only use metronome markings at a later stage. If you leave the tempo marking blank, Sibelius will default the tempo to 100 bpm.

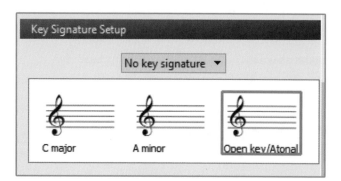

Above: It is possible to go for a No key signature option.

Key Signature Setup

Add the key signature here or leave it blank if necessary. This can always be changed later in the process. If writing for a transposing instrument, such as a trumpet, you should assume you're writing at concert pitch with a view to transposing later. With transposing instruments, there is also the choice to include a No key signature version.

SCORE INFORMATION SETUP

If you're the composer, you can happily place your name in this section. Include any information about the piece in here for your records, for example, the aesthetic of the score, or your personal enjoyment.

CREATE TITLE PAGE

You have the opportunity to create a title page at this stage that will include information about your score. While it is good to include a title page, perhaps create it later in the process, as it will be one less page to navigate while working.

APPLICATION OVERVIEW

Once you've created your score, this is the view that you'll see. It might seem a little daunting, but if you work methodically through Sibelius, you'll be reaching for the right tools in no time.

RIBBON TOOLS

The ribbon is the bar at the top of the app from which most decisions will be made (see the diagram below). All features are organized by function so that you can quickly find your way around the software. You want to add slur? That's in the Notations > Lines category. There's absolutely everything you'll ever need to create a professional-looking score in here. Scroll through or type into the search bar in the top-right corner.

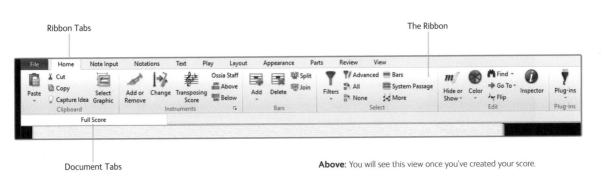

Above: You will see this view once you've created your score.

Left: If the ribbon mysteriously disappears, retrieve it via the green down arrow in the top-right corner of your screen.

PLUGINS

Some sections of the ribbon tool have plugins. These are tools that are designed to speed up your workflow in many different ways, from Quarter Tone Playback in the Play tab, to the adding of Schenkerian scalic degrees in the Review tab.

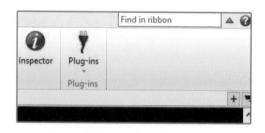

Above: The many and varied plugins will speed up various aspects of your score-writing. Explore them to find out what is on offer.

COLOURS

Different colour schemes are used to communicate various messages to the user. At first, it might seem a little confusing, but with time it'll become second nature.

Selection

Sibelius will colour any primary object selection blue. You can select multiple objects by holding Command and clicking or pressing the first selection and holding Shift and clicking the final item you'd like selected, turning them all blue.

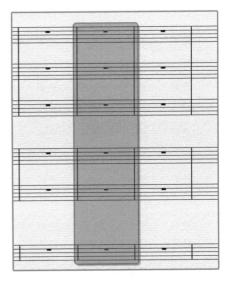

Above: Selecting a bar via Command turns it purple.

Hot Tip

To disable a selection, press the Escape key.

Selecting Multiple Bars

Select multiple bars simultaneously by holding Shift and clicking any horizontal selection. Vertical bar selections will turn the bar purple, accessed by holding Command and clicking. This will allow you to copy and paste the bar through right-clicking or Command + C > Command + V, or delete it. Holding Shift and clicking while the bar is highlighted purple will allow for multiple selections of this nature.

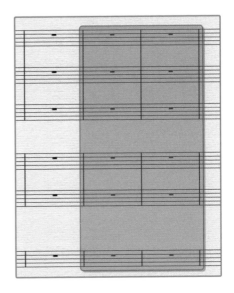

Above: A multiple bar selection. Be careful you don't accidentally delete anything!

Hot Tip

Once you've created a selection of this sort, you can only select full bars thereafter.

Instrument Range

Red noteheads suggest they're out of the range of the instrument, or difficult to play. If the latter, you will still hear the note in playback. This is particularly helpful for writing idiomatic vocal, woodwind or brass lines. Of course, discretion is advised!

Above: Suggestions such as this will help you write idiomatically for each instrument.

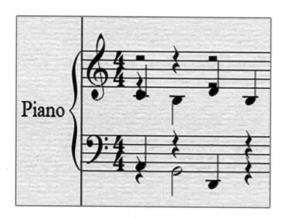

Above: Use the correct voice, otherwise confusion will ensue.

Instrument Voice

A voice is a single line. When instruments can have multiple voices on a single stave, such as piano or a SATB choral score, Sibelius can change the colour of each selected note to discern which voice it belongs to. This ensures correct stem and beam configurations and is more aesthetically pleasing. You can divide each stave into four voices as shown on the keypad (accessed through View > Keypad), ordered blue, green, orange and pink.

Hot Tip

Always make sure you're using the correct voice. Not doing so will create combinations of rests and tied notes that can make the score look confusing. You don't want your score to be unclear!

VIEWS

Change how you view the score to best suit your workflow.

① SCORE VIEW

The default view is linked to how you set up your document. It will be viewed as read when printed. Through the View tab, you can choose to spread your pages horizontally or vertically, dictating in which direction the pages move when playing back the score.

> **Hot Tip**
>
> Change your document's viewing options to a vertical page spread – **View > Pages > Vertical** – to easily scroll without losing your place while listening back to your music.

Score View ①   Panoramic View ②   Zoom ③

Below: You will be presented with a similar looking page when you've set up your score.

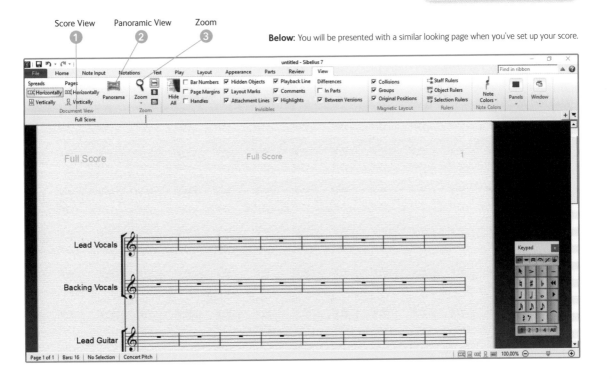

❷ PANORAMIC VIEW

This view is exactly as described. You view your score as one long horizontal document, with no page breaks. This might also help you think of your work as one long piece of music, rather than multiple sections that might be broken into pages.

Above: The shortcut to enter panoramic view is Shift + P, and all different view options are available at the bottom-right of the screen.

❸ ZOOM

There are multiple options to zoom into certain elements of your score. In the bottom-right of the screen, there is a +/- scroller that allows you to click or drag to your preferred zoom level.

Above: The options for zooming in and out of your score.

Most zooming is completed by Command + scrolling. If you get lost, visit View > Zoom, where there are multiple zoom options, selectable via a percentage in a dropdown menu, or three preset zoom levels – 100%, full-page zoom out or a quick zoom into the bar on which you're working. If you have the Zoom option enabled here, you can click and drag your mouse to zoom in.

SCORE NAVIGATION

Click and drag on a page to navigate through the score. Alternatively, you can open the navigator through View > Panels > Navigator, showing a miniature version of your score that you can click or drag to navigate through it.

You can also use the transport bar to travel through your score, found in View > Panels > Transport.

OTHER VIEWING OPTIONS

You can view more features in Sibelius that will help develop and perfect your score.

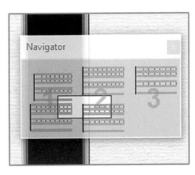

Above: The score navigator.

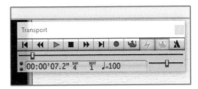

Above: The transport bar.

Below: Extra viewing options allow you to take a more pragmatic approach to the design of your score.

Invisibles ①   Rulers ②   Panels ③   Window ④

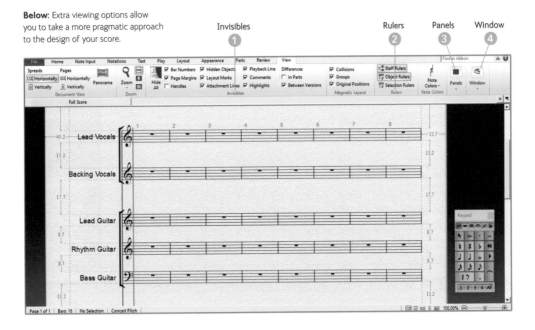

1 Invisibles

Invisibles – accessed through View > Invisibles – come in handy while editing, and are shown only to you; they're not printed in the final score. Add bar numbers to every bar, view page margins, hidden objects and more.

2 Rulers

Rulers – View > Rulers – also help score design. Every object has its conventional place in the score, to which Sibelius will automatically default. Should you wish to change anything, the rulers ensure you're lining everything up correctly.

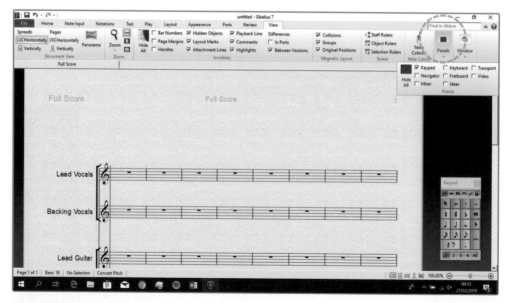

Above: Use the Panels section to speed up the process of creating a score.

3 Panels

These offer different options to help work through the score as quickly as possible and include:

- **Keypad**: Your means of inputting notes.

- **Keyboard**: Bring up a multi-octave keyboard to help you work through ideas and input notes.

- **Transport**: Play your score back here.

- **Navigator**: A bird's-eye view of the score.

- **Fretboard**: The keyboard but for guitarists.

- **Video**: If you're writing to video, view and control it here.

- **Mixer**: Balance the levels of each instrument during playback.

- **Ideas**: Save ideas for later or access over 7,000 pre-made ideas for inspiration.

4 Window

The Window options allow for multiple Sibelius scores to be open and worked on simultaneously and can be arranged as follows:

- **New Window**: Open a new instance of the score that's already open.

- **Tile Vertically**: Order all open scores from top to bottom.

- **Tile Horizontally**: Order all open scores from left to right.

- **Full Screen**: Maximize your score, hiding taskbars and minimizing any distractions.

- **Switch Windows**: Jump quickly between scores that you already have open.

SETTING UP A MIDI KEYBOARD

MIDI can bring realism and speed to your workflow. Setting up a MIDI controller is extremely easy in Sibelius and using it is easy too.

HOW TO SET UP YOUR MIDI KEYBOARD

Follow these steps to pair your keyboard with your system:

1. Connect your MIDI keyboard to your system with USB A to B or traditional MIDI cables. USB A goes into the computer and USB B goes into the keyboard. It is best to close Sibelius before you do this.

Above: You can connect your MIDI controller to Sibelius via traditional MIDI connections or USB A-B.

2. If it's the first time the MIDI device has been used on your system, expect to have to install the drivers that came with it. This will be done automatically or you will have to download them from the proprietary website, depending on your computer and device.

3. Re-open your score.

4. Check your device is available in Note Input > Input Devices and ensure the computer is receiving the signal by playing the keys and checking that the Test bar lights up green in accordance with the velocity of your notes. You are now set up.

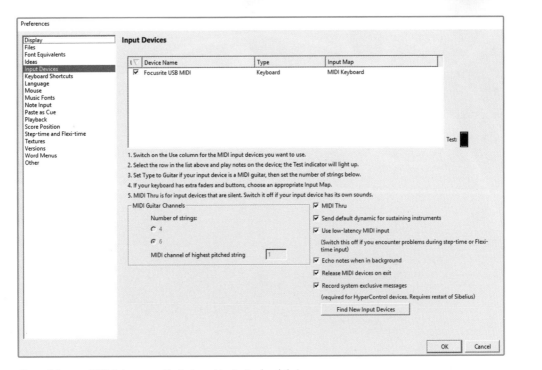

Above: Select your MIDI device, ensure Sibelius is receiving its signal, and play!

NOTE ENTRY

ENTERING NOTES

Enter notes into your score through your computer keypad or MIDI. Using both the keypad and MIDI is a sure-fire way to work quickly in Sibelius. Once it's in your muscle memory, you and your scores will benefit hugely from your new-found skills.

NOTE ENTRY TOOL

The main tool for adding notes is the keypad. The first page consists of note lengths; click the duration you'd like and click to position the note on the score. Continue placing notes without re-clicking the keypad if they're the same duration as what's already been selected.

Left: The keypad will become your best friend.

The Caret

The caret is a blue line that shows where you're about to place a note. If it disappears, Press N to make it reappear.

Above: The caret will visually guide your note placement.

Adding Accidentals

Accidentals can be placed alongside notes by selecting the appropriate accidental in the keypad. After this, choose the note duration you would like and place the note on the stave. If you'd like to add the accidental after you've created the note, select the note > accidental on the keypad.

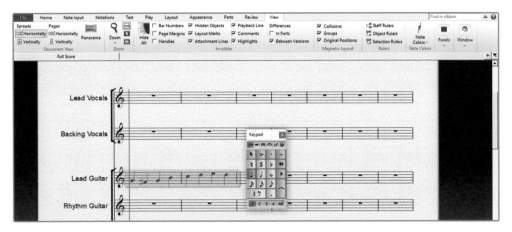

Above: Adding accidentals to notes is as simple as a couple of clicks. Remember that the accidentals are only needed if the notes are outside those suggested in the key signature.

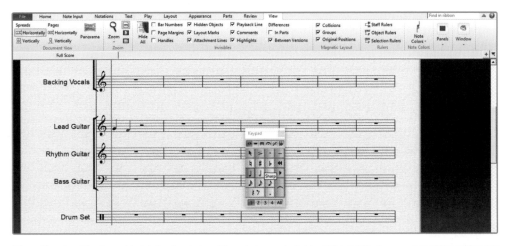

Above: If you're adding the accidental after the placing of the note, be sure to first tap ESC to tell Sibelius you aren't adding another note.

Adding Two or More Notes

Adding two or more vertically related notes will require the last note to remain active as shown by the caret. If the caret is inactive, the first note will have to be re-inputted, after which you can place the second note.

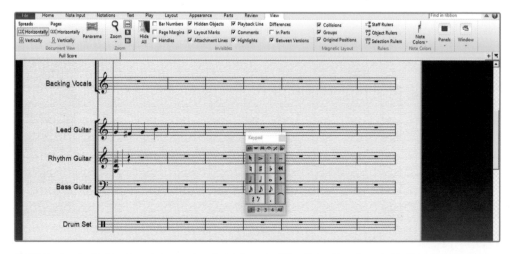

Above: If a greyed-out note appears where your mouse is placed, you should be able to add another note; the blue note shown here is the last note to have been placed.

Adding Bars

After a while, it will become necessary to add bars. The shortcut Command + B will add a bar to the end of the score, as will Home > Bars > Add. From the drop-down menu, you can add a single, multiple or irregular bars at any selected point.

Left: Adding multiple bars is easy with the drop-down menu.

Deleting Bars

Similarly, go to Home > Bars > Delete and selected bars will be deleted upon confirmation of a dialog box. As mentioned, hold Command + click the bar, turning the bar purple, and press Delete or Backspace on your keyboard. This will not ask you to confirm the action, so make sure you're deleting the right thing.

Hot Tip

If you make a mistake, there's an undo button located in the top-left of the screen, or just press Command + Z.

Triplets

Triplets can be added by clicking a note duration you'd like to convert and selecting Note Input > Triplets. Converting a selected note will create three iterations of said note; a single crotchet would become three, equivalent to the length of a minim. Any constituent note durations can be used from this point, providing there's space in the triplet. If you'd like to fit nine

Above: Triplets can help to change the feel of the metre of your music.

demisemiquavers into the space of a crotchet, you must first input a demisemiquaver, then select Nonuplet in the Triplet dialog box.

Cross Staff Notes

For grand-staved instruments it's common to join the staves through cross staff notes. To input these, create the phrase in a single stave with parts that might overlap, select Note Input > Cross Staff Notes, and select whether you'd like the beam to be above or below. You can also use the shortcut Command + Shift + up/down arrows.

Above: You might not know when you'll need to write cross staff notes.

COMPUTER KEYBOARD ENTRY

Using your keyboard can massively improve the speed at which you input notes.

Above: Use your keyboard to input notes quickly.

ADDING NOTES

Use the number pad on your keyboard and your mouse to place the note. Your number pad equates to Sibelius's keypad:

- **0**: Crotchet Rest

- **1**: Demisemiquaver

- **2**: Semiquaver

- **3**: Quaver

- **4**: Crotchet

- **5**: Minim

- **6**: Semibreve

- **7**: Natural Sign

- **8**: Sharp

- **9**: Flat

CHANGING PITCH

You can just as easily change the pitch using the up and down arrows. This will cause notes to move stepwise diatonically. Move multiple notes by creating a selection and using the up and down arrows.

You can also add chords by selecting the interval on the top line of numbers on the computer keyboard. 1 relates to unison, 2 a minor second and so on; 8 is an octave up. If you wish to create a second note below the original, hold Shift and select the interval. An octave below would be the key combination Shift + 8.z

Hot Tip

If you press keys 7, 8 or 9 and then a note relating to duration, you can input both note and accidental simultaneously. Using the mouse, you can select a note that has already been placed and use the keypad to change its properties.

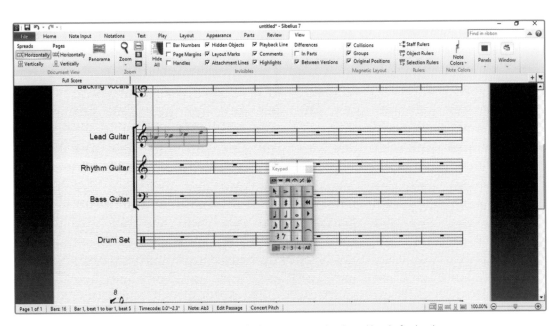

Above: Be careful with moving some selections. In this instance the C♭ was not required, and was able to be fixed easily.

OTHER MODES OF NOTE ENTRY

There are other ways to enter notes into your score, including via MIDI or via the visual interface of an instrument.

MIDI ENTRY

If you've already connected your MIDI device, then you're ready to input notes through MIDI. There are two main ways to do this: through recording a performance directly into the notation software, or guiding the note selection of already determined note values with the keyboard, as previously described.

MIDI Record Entry

You can press Record in the transport bar to begin the count-in. After one bar, the recording will begin. Be careful to get the

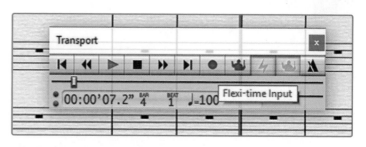

Above: Change the tempo and press the record button to get your count-in.

note duration as precise as possible; Sibelius will record the MIDI as played, meaning that some unusual lengths of notes might be seen. Try to make sure each note is articulated, to avoid unnecessary stacks of notes, rather than what should have been a phrase of separate notes.

Hot Tip

Try recording with a low buffer size first, and also with the tempo much slower than written. This means that if you are copying a score, you can sight-read with ease and therefore make fewer mistakes.

Above: Go a bit slower and avoid misreadings such as these!

Keyboard Entry

It is possible to input notes without recording. Via the keypad you can specify the note duration and enter the note via the keyboard. This is especially useful during periods that have lots of repeated rhythms – it's much quicker than drawing in all of the notes yourself.

Hot Tip

Create interesting textures with the pitch and modulation controls on your keyboard, adding an extra dimension to your score. Be sure to notate these too.

VIRTUAL PIANO ENTRY

Through View > Panels > Keyboard, you can add notes using the virtual piano. As with previous modes of input, select the duration of the desired note and then press the piano key. This makes it quicker for those notes with multiple ledger lines that might become confusing.

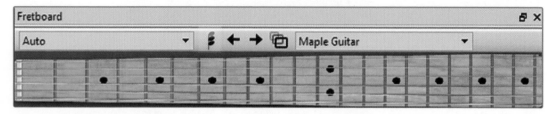

Above: The visual element of inputting notes via a keyboard or fretboard can make for quicker and more accurate note entry.

VIRTUAL FRETBOARD ENTRY

Through View > Panels > Fretboard, you can do the exact same thing, this time adding notes using a virtual acoustic or electric guitar, or a four-string or five-string electric bass. This helps guitarists who may not be able to read music, but know what rhythms they're playing, to input scores.

Hot Tip

It is not advisable to record through the clicks of a mouse unless it's at an extremely slow tempo, or you're amazingly accurate with a mouse.

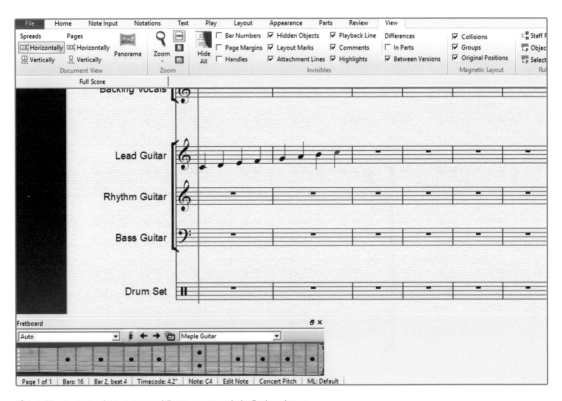

Above: It's easy to translate your guitar skills into a score with the Fretboard view.

PERCUSSION

Percussion scores require slightly different staves to others. There are single-staved instruments, five-line percussion staves and pitched percussion staves. Whatever you need, Sibelius will have multiple options for you.

OVERVIEW

If you need a percussion stave, select it in the Instrument Setup menu at the start of the score, or add it via Home > Instruments > Add or Remove, and use the menu.

Hot Tip

Make sure you've got the right percussion stave for your instrument.

Above: The three different types of percussion staves: one for pitched percussion, with a clef to dictate pitch; a single line, notating only rhythm; and a five-line, for multiple instruments, such as a drum set.

NOTE ENTRY

Note entry for percussion instruments is completed in the same way as melodic instruments, through the keypad, clicking or MIDI. Be aware that noteheads for percussion are slightly different. For example, cymbals tend to make use of crosses as noteheads, and the rest of a drum kit might be scored out on the stave. If you're used to programming drums in a Digital Audio Workstation, it would be worth recording a few ideas just as you would in a DAW, and see how the notation is set up.

Hot Tip

If drummer is playing with two limbs simultaneously, i.e, playing a hi-hat and snare at the same time, then the note stems should point different ways.

Above: Take note of the style of notation here. Cymbals are represented by Xs, while drums are signified by actual notes. From top to bottom: Crash Cymbal, Ride Cymbal, Closed Hi Hat, Snare drum, Toms (pitched high to low), Bass drum.

TABLATURE

Tablature is a type of notation used for popular plucked string instruments, like guitars, bass guitar, ukulele and lutes. It is generally shortened to tab and is a representation of the finger patterns and shapes used by guitarists.

OVERVIEW

Guitar notation tends to include both tablature and conventional notation. This means that you might have to add two separate instruments in the setup menu and group them together manually if you have more than one guitar part.

Hot Tip

You will notice that above each number there is a rhythm beam, just as is found on a traditional stave.

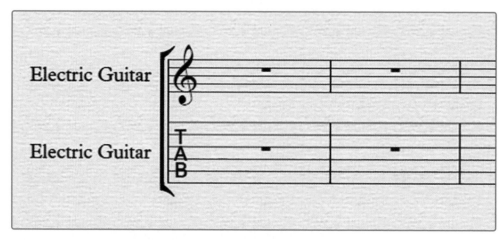

Above: How a contemporary guitar part should look at the beginning.

TAB ENTRY

If you're wanting to write tablature but are unsure about where to start, you can first write the conventional notation and copy it into the tablature stave. Sibelius automatically maps out the position of the notes on the fretboard, but try to check this, if possible.

If you know the fret, select the note duration on the keypad and click the fret in the Fretboard view, or type it in when prompted by the caret.

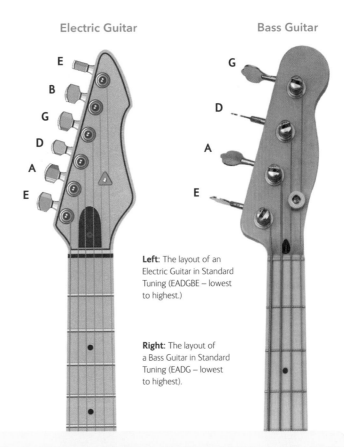

Electric Guitar   Bass Guitar

Left: The layout of an Electric Guitar in Standard Tuning (EADGBE – lowest to highest.)

Right: The layout of a Bass Guitar in Standard Tuning (EADG – lowest to highest).

Hot Tip

When writing for a guitarist, be sure to check the fretboard diagrams above to help you decide what's the most comfortable for a guitarist to play. Check out orchestration manuals and online video clips of demonstrations of the guitar to make sure you're also getting the sound you're hearing in your head.

ADDING DETAIL TO YOUR SCORE

ADD TO YOUR SCORE

To get a truly great sound from your musicians, it's not just the notes you put on the score. You need to tell the musicians how to perform it, how to articulate the music.

ARTICULATIONS

Articulations tell a performer how to play a note, generally shown as symbols placed above or below the stave. They add more interesting sounds to the music, therefore creating more potential to show emotion.

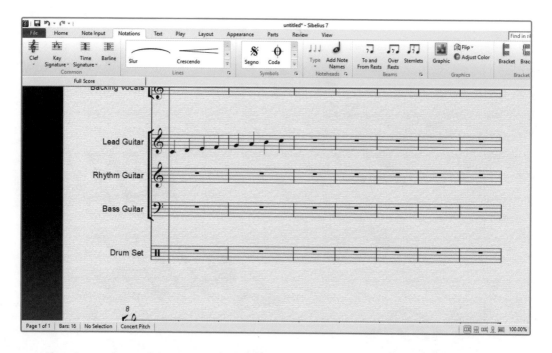

Above: Insert any line or symbol on to any part of your score from here. If choosing an object without a prior score selection, you can select the object to place, and click anywhere in the score to place it.

Above: You can find articulations on most tabs of the keypad.

Adding an Articulation From the Keypad

You can add an articulation when inputting a note on the keypad. If you know the symbol that you need, press the note duration, choose the articulation and input the note. The articulations feature on the top row of the first tab, but there are more on the later tabs on the keypad.

Articulations From the Ribbon

You can add articulations from the ribbon via Notation > Lines or Symbols. Highlight the note and select the preferred articulation and it will appear. These are ordered by definition and where they're most likely to be used, so if you're looking for a percussion symbol, you know to search Notation > Symbol > Percussion.

Above: Articulations change the performance of a note.

TEXT

Text in Sibelius is essential to communicate thoughts to the musician. Whether it's lyrics, a brief to a score or notes on a technique, they're all helpful. You don't need to write them in traditional Italian either!

OVERVIEW

Text can be added via right-clicking + Text > choosing a drop-down option > inputting text. Other options can also be found in Text on the ribbon.

LYRICS

Lyrics in Sibelius can be added via Text > Lyrics, or Command + L after selecting a note on the score.

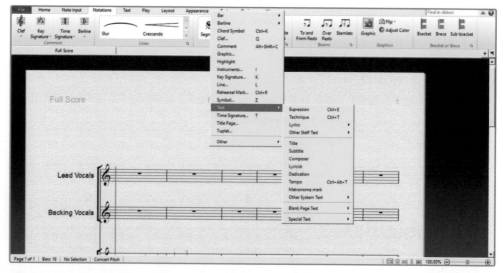

Above: Choose to input any text option, select where you'd like it placed, and Sibelius will format it to its conventional default position.

Adding Lyrics

Scores tend to work syllabically, although you may find instances where one syllable is written for many notes – this is called melisma. Where you only need one note per word, simply type the word and press space to move on. If a word has more than one syllable, it is necessary to hyphenate the word and create the extra note.

Above: Words broken into their constituent syllables are connected by a hyphen.

Hot Tip

If you'd like to create a melisma, create the notes, type the first syllable and then press space for each note that you would like the melisma to last. All notes in the melisma should be grouped together with a legato mark.

Create Lyrics From Text File

Text file

Click Browse to choose the text file containing the lyrics you want to add to the score:

[   ]

Browse...

Language

Lyrics are in: English ▼

☑ Automatically syllabify ambiguous words

Appearance

Lyrics text style: Lyrics line 1 ▼

☑ Delete existing lyrics first

☑ Use apostrophes to show combined syllables

☑ Warn when lyrics won't fit the music

OK   Cancel

Above: It is usually not necessary to change any options in this dialog box.

Import From Text File

You can import lyrics from text files (.txt). Select the passage you'd like to include a lyric for, go to Text > Lyric > Import From Text File > Browse, select the file and press OK. Upon selecting the language, Sibelius will automatically syllabify your text and attach it to the pre-written notes.

Hot Tip

When you import text, make sure your notes match the number of syllables ready to be imported.

TECHNIQUE

Technique marks are placed above the score and created by selecting the object, then Command + T. Type in the technique once the cursor appears (all lower-case), or right-click and select from the drop-down menu. You can right-click and select the technique and place it yourself, if you would prefer to not use the shortcut. The marking should snap to the conventional position above the notehead.

Adding Expression

Expressions can be added in a similar way to techniques, although the shortcut is Command + E. If text, you can type this when the cursor appears and the text will appear italicized.

arco	.	Ctrl+.	û
con sord.	←	Ctrl+[	ù
div.	→	Ctrl+]	À
divisi	♫		Á
l.v.	♪		Ç
mute	♪		È
nat.	♪		É
open			Ì
pizz.		Ctrl+3	Í
senza sord.	♩	Ctrl+Alt+9	Ò
solo	+	Ctrl+Alt+7	Ó
sul pont.		Ctrl+Alt+8	Ù
sul tasto	┼	Ctrl+Alt++	Ú
tre corde	à	Ctrl+Alt+Shift+A	Û
tremolo	á	Ctrl+Shift+A	Û
tutti	ä		ß
una corda	å		·	Alt+'
unis.	å		'	Alt+Shift+'
♯		ç	Ctrl+Alt+Shift+E	"	Alt+2
♯	Ctrl+7	è	Ctrl+Shift+E	"	Alt+Shift+2
♯	Ctrl+8	é	—
♭	Ctrl+9	ê	
x		ë	
♭♭		ì	
♪		í	
♪	Ctrl+1	ï	
♪	Ctrl+2	î	
♩	Ctrl+3	ô	Ctrl+Alt+Shift+O
♩	Ctrl+4	ó	Ctrl+Shift+O
♩	Ctrl+5	õ	
♩	Ctrl+6	ô	
∞		ù	
⋈		ú	Ctrl+Alt+Shift+U
⋈		û	Ctrl+Shift+U

Above: There are many techniques available to be selected through a few short clicks.

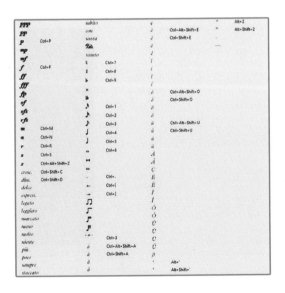

Left: The various options for expression text in Sibelius. You can also type your own.

Dynamics

You can add performance dynamics through the creation of an expression. From the Expression drop-down menu, you see the keyboard shortcuts for each dynamic. You can select a passage and a dynamic range.

Hot Tip

You can type in the dynamics to your score, but they will not be emboldened as is standard practice.

ADDING ARTICULATIONS TO SECTIONS

Should you wish to add an articulation, technique or expression to a whole passage, highlight the passage and add the feature. If it's an articulation, it will show on the noteheads of all selected notes. Techniques and notes will show above or under the first selected note. Toggle between notehead articulations by repeatedly pressing the same button on the

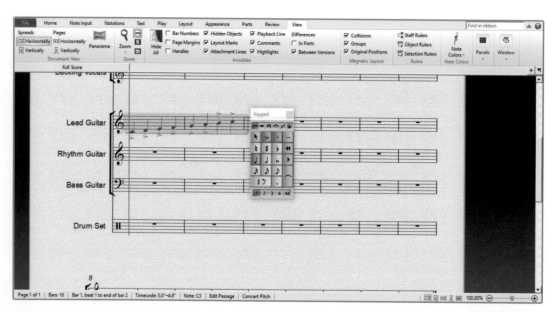

Above: The most common articulations are found on the keypad. Add staccato, accents or tenuto markings from the first page.

keypad. If some notes in a selected passage already have the articulation, one press will add the articulation to the remaining noteheads, another will remove them all.

REHEARSAL MARKS

Split the music into sections that are easier to rehearse by selecting the object above which you'd like the mark and click Text > Rehearsal Marks, or use the shortcut Command + R.

Above: Split your score into manageable sections with Rehearsal marks.

TEXT COMMENTS

Comments add an extra dimension of communication between composer and performer and can state what you would like out of the music. Make a comment via right-click > Text > Special Text > Comment.

CHANGING KEYS, TIME AND BARLINES

Changing the key signature, time signature or including a barline is just as easy as adding or deleting a bar.

CHANGING THE KEY SIGNATURE

You can change the key signature at any point in the score and Sibelius will add any necessary double barlines around this. You can select the bar and type K, giving you a dropdown menu, from which you can select the key. You can also access this drop-down menu by highlighting the bar and going to Notations > Common > Key Signature.

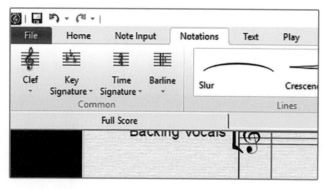

Above: The area to change keys, time and barlines.

If you've already written material before the key signature change, Sibelius will change the accidentals present on all notes after the new key signature. The score will be enharmonically correct, just not written as well as you might like. Delete a key signature by selecting it and hitting Delete on your keypad.

CHANGING THE TIME SIGNATURE

Change the time signature of a bar by selecting the bar and pressing T. Select or type in your desired time signature. The change will be placed on anything selected. You can delete the time signature change by selecting the signature and pressing Delete. Sibelius will present you with a dialog box, asking if you'd like to rewrite the bars for the rest of the score. Click Yes and the score will be changed to the new time signature.

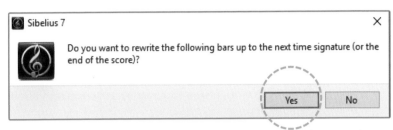

Above: Click Yes to roll out your new time signature change across the score.

ADDING BARLINES

Change a barline by selecting the line you'd like changed and going to Notations > Common > Barline. Create repeat sections, dotted barlines and more.

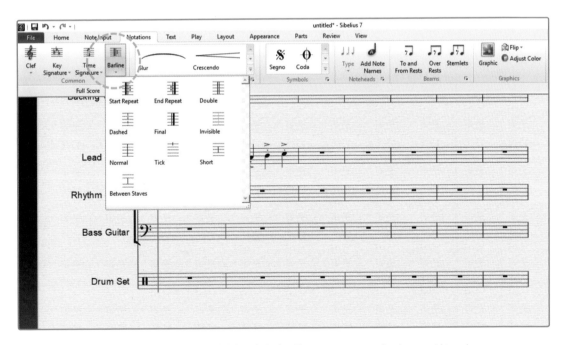

Above: Change multiple barlines by holding Ctrl/Cmd and clicking the barline. There are many options for what you might need in the barline section of Notations.

REPEAT MARKINGS

Repeat markings can sometimes be confusing. When thinking about first and second endings, and where to jump to after certain sections, it's difficult to know where to start.

OVERVIEW

Luckily, Sibelius makes it rather easy to figure out how we'd like to insert our repeats. Repeat markings can make the score smaller, more efficient, and can be helpful when we don't have a lot of time to score out huge sections over again.

CREATING THE REPEAT

Repeats can be added by selecting the barline you'd like changed and visiting Notation > Common > Barline. Depending on your position in the repeat, you can insert a Start Repeat or End Repeat.

Left: Make sure to select the correct barline for your repeat markings.

FIRST AND SECOND ENDINGS

These are just as easy to add in Sibelius and it's always nice when you hear it played back. First and Second Endings are found in Notation > Line > Repeat Endings. Before the repeat barline, select the length of the ending and select the necessary line. Once placed, you can select the remaining material and select Second Ending. The end repeat must be in place before playback is heard.

Above: First and Second endings are a great way of remaining efficient and reducing page counts in your score, as shown here.

SLURS, HAIRPINS AND OTHER SHAPES

Music notation is full of shapes of different sizes that all serve a function of communication in some way.

Above: All of these shapes have a meaning related to performance.

Below: Find some extra shapes on the keypad's fifth tab.

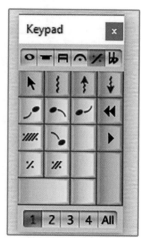

OVERVIEW

Save space in your score by adding shapes rather than longer items of text. Add shapes to a selection by visiting Notation > Lines or Symbols. This can include legato markings, pedal markings for piano players and more.

FROM THE KEYPAD

Some shapes are available from the keypad. If you're writing for trumpet, for example, scoops and falls can be found in the keypad's fifth tab.

FROM LINES

Other shapes are available from Notation > Lines.
Select the shape and it will be applied to your score.

Hot Tip

The shortcut for the
line section is L.

LEGATO MARKING

You can highlight a whole section and click Legato/Slur from the Lines box to create a
legato mark over the whole selection. Alternatively, you can also select or write legato as an
expression. This is commonly used, so is therefore the first option in the Lines window.
You can also select a single note, hit Slur and it will automatically format a slur that connects

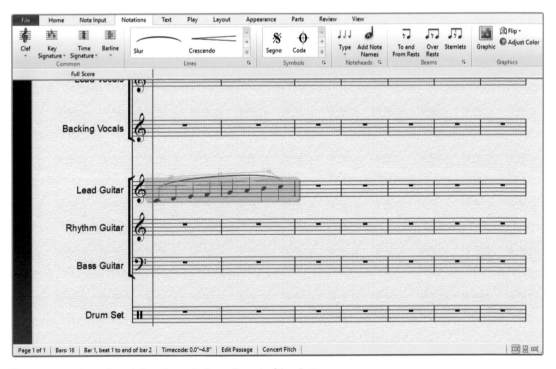

Above: Legato markings will attach themselves to the first and last note of the selection.

to the following note. You cannot create legato marks for multiple instruments at the same time.

HAIRPINS

You can add a hairpin to show an increase or decrease in amplitude. Make a selection and select the hairpin from Notation > Line. If a change in volume is needed over a longer period of time, it may be neater to type the expression cresc. or dim. under the selected passage.

Hot Tip

Place a dynamic marking after the hairpin so performers are aware of how much the volume should change during the performance of the shape.

Above: It is preferable to keep hairpins to a maximum length of two bars.

EDITING SHAPES

Sometimes shapes will need editing to fit into the score.

ANCHOR POINTS

Anchor points are small, blue boxes that signify moveable points of a shape that allow you to edit an object. Common ways of editing shapes are extending lines to cover longer passages of music and editing the length and angle of a slur. You can drag the box or click and use the arrow keys to move it in any direction.

Hot Tip

You can extend shapes over pages by clicking and dragging the anchor point. You should then release your mouse in the desired area.

Above: If a shape has not appeared exactly how you would have liked, you can easily edit it through the options available in Sibelius.

COPYING AND PASTING SHAPES

If you want to use the same shape across multiple staves, select the shape and press Command + C to copy, then click and press Command + V where you'd like the object pasted.

Above: All objects have anchor points that allow you to edit them in any way you wish.

MAKING CHANGES TO MULTIPLE STAVES

Some shapes may affect a whole score. For example, a fermata placed on a stave will change Sibelius's global playback, but it is still necessary to paste the marking on all performers' parts. Highlight all the bars in which you'd like the shapes to be placed (in this case by Command + clicking) and select the shape on the keypad.

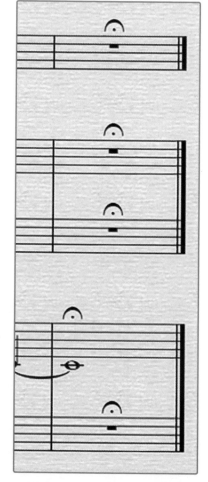

Right: Make sure global directions are added to everyone's score!

IMPORTING GRAPHICS

Sibelius can import graphics for you to use in your score, whether as an avant-garde graphic instruction or as decoration to fill blank space.

ACCEPTED FORMATS

Multiple types of graphic are now accepted, including BMP, GIF, JPG, TIFF and SVB (Scalable Vector Graphic). To import, right-click > Graphic, choose your graphic and import.

Editing Graphics

Much like shapes, graphics can also be edited through anchor points. Once you've edited your graphic, you can use the anchor points to rotate it to any angle, scale it or crop it. You can change its colour, brightness, contrast and opacity, just as in other visual editing software.

Right: Edit your graphics in a similar way to other photo-editing software.

Above: Fill space and make your score more engaging by including a graphic.

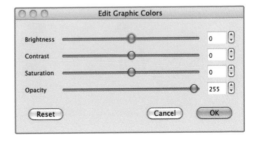

ADDING CHORDS

In more popular styles of music it may be more efficient to only write a melody and accompanying chords, allowing for easier distribution and improvised arrangements.

OVERVIEW

Add chords through the Text tab manually or make use of Sibelius's smart technology and have it create the chords for you.

CHORD INPUT

To add a chord symbol to your score, first choose Text > Chord Symbol. If you've already highlighted a bar above which you'd like to place the chord, a text marker will appear; if not, select the place you'd like it. You can either right-click or type the name of the chord, which will automatically be formatted by Sibelius.

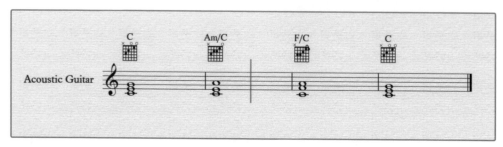

Above: Sibelius's smart technology helps to create chord diagrams more quickly.

ADD FROM NOTES

You can direct Sibelius to analyse the notes and add chords as appropriate. Make a selection and choose Create from notes, proceeding through the dialog box. If you're working off guitar-based notation, you can select Guitar Scale Diagram to show the chord diagram on a fretboard. Select the bar, select the feature and tell Sibelius what guitar is in use, thus creating idiomatic parts.

Above: Keep your score contemporary, help out your performers and provide the opportunity for an embellished arrangement by providing chord symbols rather than specific notation to your melody.

OTHER OPTIONS FOR CHORDS

Sibelius can analyse and suggest chord names for those used in the score, but it's not always 100 per cent accurate. You can use the following features to rectify any errors or suggest any intricacies to other musicians to aid their performance.

Equivalent Chord Spellings

If a misspelled chord appears, you can press Equivalent Chord Text (or Command + Shift + K) and the chord will be rearranged. You can also tell Sibelius to respell the chord if, for example,

Above: Sibelius is generally correct when analysing the chords inputted into the score, but if there is a misreading (as in the top diagram), change it without having to restart the whole analysis process.

you are playing in a sharp-based key, but the chord should be written as flat. Respell Chord Text will fix this for you. Keep selecting until it is correct.

Editing Chord Diagrams

If you're aware of how to play a certain chord, or want to use a certain voicing, specify it in the score by selecting the chord diagram and hitting Respell Chord Diagram. Cycle through the options and choose the preferred result. Do it manually via clicking finger positions in Edit Chord Diagram.

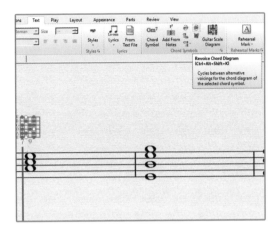

Above: On stringed instruments, the position at which notes are played on the strings can change timbre. If you're aware of this and have a specific idea of where the performer should position themselves on their instrument, you can dictate it here.

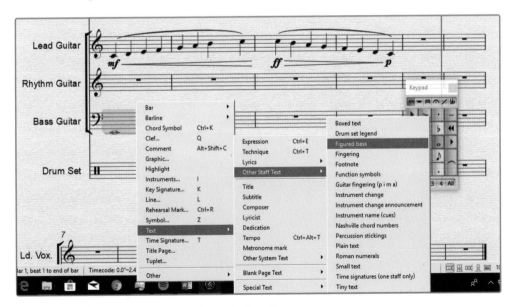

Above: Create opportunities for new arrangements by providing figured bass.

EDITING YOUR SCORE

PERFECTING YOUR SCORE

> After inputting the notes, the next job is to format the score to make it look as professional as possible.

EDITING OVERVIEW

Editing your score could include anything from the correct spacing of staves and systems, to the more 'formal' aspects of written text, including a title page, composer's notes or even copyright notices. The overarching features that help you in this department are found in the Layout tab.

Below: Most features to create a professional-looking score are found here.

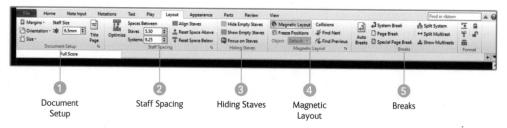

1 Document Setup
2 Staff Spacing
3 Hiding Staves
4 Magnetic Layout
5 Breaks

❶ DOCUMENT SETUP

Margins
The first aspect of the Layout tab is Margins (found in Layout > Document Setup). The wider the margin, the more you can fit on a page.

Orientation
You can change whether your page setup is portrait or landscape through Document Setup > Orientation. If creating a blank score, the default page orientation is portrait.

Hot Tip

Changing the staff size will significantly affect other elements of your page's layout.

Size

The size of the score can be set via a template found in Document Setup > Size.

Staff Size

By default, the Sibelius staff size is 7 mm. This can be changed in Document Setup > Staff Size, through the use of the arrow, or by typing it in.

Title Page

Create a title page after you've started your score. Do so with Layout > Title Page. Creating a title, whether on a title page or at the top of your score, is done by right-clicking > Text > Title.

Hot Tip

You can reformat your text by changing elements found in Text > Format.

Full Score	Full Score	1
	A PIECE	
A. Lyricist		A. Composer
		arr. A. Arranger

Above: Lyricist information goes on the left of the score, while composers appear on the right, with arranger underneath.

○ **Composer/arranger info**: Lyricist and composer information is placed at the top of your score on the left and right respectively. To add this, right-click > Text > Composer. Sibelius will automatically place the text. To create a line break between composer and arranger, hit Enter after inserting the first piece of text.

○ **Tempo text**: Include a metronome mark to dictate the tempo of a score in beats per minute (BPM). To do so, right-click > Text > Metronome Mark to bring up the cursor. From here, right-click and select the preferred beat to which you're counting, then type = and your tempo.

Hot Tip

If using a compound time signature (6/8, for example), make sure you add the dot to signify the beat, or Sibelius's player will count it incorrectly!

Above: In this example, the performers are instructed to perform the music at 100 crotchets a minute. Note the marking is attached to the first bar of the score – move it by dragging.

❷ STAFF SPACING

Spaces Between Staves/Systems

With spaces between staves and systems, you can manually enter your preferred spacing, or click a stave on the score and drag it up or down. Make sure you can still read everything clearly!

Optimize

Optimize sets all staff spacing and line breaks, and moves shapes to where Sibelius believes is best. To apply to the whole score, press Command + A > Layout > Optimize. If nothing is selected, Sibelius will present a dialog box suggesting it's applied to the whole score.

> ### Hot Tip
>
> **A simple way to check whether your score is properly spaced is to check Collisions. Click Magnetic Layout > Collisions > Find Next/ Previous to jump to a part of the score with overlapping dynamics, or other elements that Sibelius has deemed to be colliding.**

Below: This is what an excerpt of a score might look like pre-optimization, in which some elements of the score are bunched up; see next page for optimized version. See the next page for a post-optimized version.

Above: Post-optimization, your score will look much neater, with extra space given to certain score elements, such as the chord diagram and dynamic markings.

③ HIDING STAVES

Hide Empty Staves

You can hide certain staves if there's nothing written for an extended amount of time. Select a passage of score, then Layout > Hide Empty Staves. You can show all instruments on the first page, then highlight the rest of the score and hide the empty staves. When the instruments are due to return, give a four-bar cue so they're able to count in.

④ MAGNETIC LAYOUT

All objects attached to the score have optimal positions on the page. Magnetic Layout will ensure they stick to their proprietary notes and repel others, leaving the score as clean as possible. This is accessed through Layout > Magnetic Layout.

Hot Tip

Freeze the positions of elements by selecting the passage and hitting Layout > Magnetic Layout > Freeze Positions. They're now locked into place.

⑤ BREAKS

Breaks and Staves

Should you not be satisfied with Sibelius's suggestions for stave breaks, select the barline where you'd like the break to be placed and click Layout > Breaks > System Break/Page Break. You can also dictate Auto Breaks, telling Sibelius to break the system once a numerical threshold has been reached. Tick Use Auto System Breaks to do this.

System Breaks

☑ Use auto system breaks
- ○ Every `4` bars
  - ☑ If exceeded due to locked formatting, break as soon as possible
- ◉ At or before:
  - ☑ Rehearsal marks
  - ☑ Tempo text
  - ☑ Double barlines
  - ☑ Key changes
  - ☑ Multirests of `4` bars or more
  - System must be `50` % full

Multirests

☐ Use multirests
- ☐ Empty sections between final barlines: `TACET`
- ☐ Automatically split multirests:
  - ◉ Split into groups of `8` bars
  - ○ Split where bar numbers are multiples of `10`

Page Breaks

☐ Use auto page breaks
- ☐ At final barlines
- ☐ At bar rests
  - ◉ After every page
  - ○ After right-hand pages
  - After `1` or more bar rests
  - ☐ Prefer longer rest before page break
  - Page must be `60` % full
☑ Add warnings at difficult page turns
- ◉ Spectacles
- ○ Text: `V.S.`

[OK]   [Cancel]

Above: Input your preferences here to create auto breaks for your score, allowing for cleaner, better spaced-out pages.

Deleting Page Breaks

Re-attach as much of the proceeding system as possible by deleting the issued break.

Above: Delete a system break here, making the two systems into one.

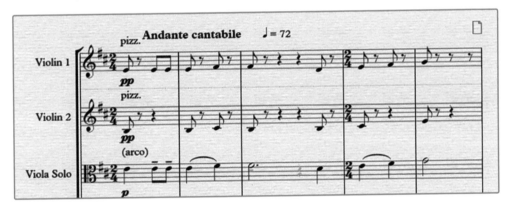

Above: Delete a page break here, combining as much of the following page as possible with the previous one.

FILTERING A SELECTION

Should you wish to edit every instance of a certain feature of your score, you can highlight them all by clicking Home > Select > Filters and choosing the feature of your choice from the drop-down menu.

FURTHER EDITING AND SCORE DESIGN

The elements already discussed will enable your score to be read by a performer. Now you can stamp it with an air of professionalism by improving its overall aesthetics.

OVERVIEW

The Appearance tab is the section where you can finalize the aesthetic element of your score. You can change the global style of the score, thus eliciting a certain playing style from your performers.

Below: The Appearance tab.

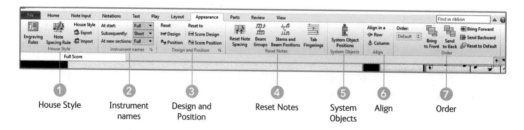

❶	❷	❸	❹	❺	❻	❼
House Style	Instrument names	Design and Position	Reset Notes	System Objects	Align	Order

❶ HOUSE STYLE

Engraving Rules
Engraving Rules allow you to change the specific elements of the score, from changing the distance between each tremolo line to the width of a slur, it's all there.

Hot Tip

Sibelius is both user- and performer-friendly. Be careful not to become overwhelmed by the minutiae and ruin the look of your score.

Note Spacing Rule

If you don't like the distance between notes, or perhaps the distance between a note and its concurrent accidental, change it via the Note Spacing Rule dialog. Notes can also be spaced manually by dragging them.

House Styles

Change the house style you set at the beginning through House Style > Import. If you're proud of the look of your score, hit Export so you can use it in other scores. Make sure to name it clearly!

Right: You can manually edit the note spacing in your score or change it in the relevant dialog box.

❷ INSTRUMENT NAMES

Sometimes the instrument name used in the final score may not match the sound heard on playback. To change an instrument name, double-click the name, bringing up the cursor, and type it in, clicking elsewhere in the score to confirm afterwards. The shortened name can be modified by selecting the instrument name in the second system, and changing it to your preferred name. This will also change the recurring instances of that name.

Above: Type in an instrument name as with any word processor, and Sibelius will format it automatically.

Instrument Name Length

Edit the length of the instrument name through Appearance > Instrument Names. The drop-down boxes allow you to change how your instrument names will appear on the score at different points.

❸ DESIGN AND POSITION

If you've moved an element and are unsure of where it should be, use the options here to reset them to their original positions. This is very similar to Optimize.

❹❺ RESET NOTES AND SYSTEM OBJECTS

Reset Notes and Other Options

You can reset said elements of the score through this method. It's particularly helpful when you've taken your manual editing too far.

⑥ ALIGN

Alignment of Elements

Elements can be aligned horizontally or vertically. As stated, most objects have a default placement, but in some instances – for example, when layering elements such as a dynamic marking or expression marking, you might

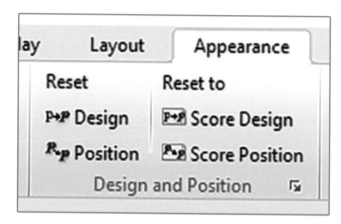

Above: Sibelius will help align elements that may seem out of place.

find they may not align to previous markings on the same stave. This can be amended here through selecting the objects and hitting the command.

⑦ ORDER

Order organises objects, mainly images, in a score from front to back. You can place an image behind staves in the score by clicking 'Send to Back', and to the front by clicking 'Bring to Front'. This can bring an extra dimension to graphics imported in your score.

BRACKET OR BRACE

A bracket groups together more than one instrument, for example, a string section – showing that they are all playing together and most commonly part of the same instrument family. A brace is a smaller bracket that ties together two staves of a musical instrument, such as a piano. The majority of the time Sibelius adds these for you, but should you choose a more eclectic group of instruments that you'd like to read together – a flute and a violin, for example – you can add the bracket by selecting a bar in each instrument, then Notations > Bracket. This will create the bracket around both instrument names. Alternatively, add the bracket to one instrument and drag the anchor point seen in the image below downwards.

Above: Drag the anchor point downwards to create your group.

THE FINAL SCORE

FINISHING UP

Great! You've got your final score! Now you might like to prepare it to be played and shared with others.

OVERVIEW

You can prepare a mix of your score and export it to send to others. This is helpful for showing what a final product might sound like. You can also export parts and send a score to others to add their feedback for further improvement.

SAVING YOUR SCORE

As with any project, it is important to remember to save your score. You can do this from File > Save As/Save and telling Sibelius where you'd like it saved. From then on, you can use Command + S as a shortcut, or clicking the floppy disk button in the upper-left corner of the software.

Backup and Auto-Save

Should Sibelius crash, auto-saves and backups exist to make sure you don't lose any work. Reload Sibelius and you should see a message asking if you'd like to re-open the score on which you were previously working. Should this not appear, backups are always saved to the Scores folder, found at:

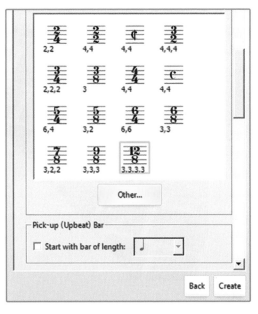

Above: Now you've got your final score, what can you do with it?

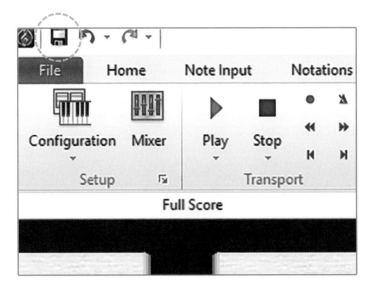

- **Windows:** C:\Users\ Your Username\ Documents\Scores

- **Mac:** MacHD > Users > Username > Documents > Scores

Left: Save your scores in a click with the floppy disk icon in the top-left corner.

Suggested File-keeping Methods

It's a good idea to keep a tidy computer and work system. It is easier to draw up old projects and keep track of how a project is running. Create a folder for every project and name it appropriately. This will have multiple names until the final score is completed, after which you can rename the folder with the title of the work.

Save your files in a way that's easy to find and track its progress at a later date:

○ **Date** [YYYYMMDD]–Name [what the project reminds you of]–Key–Tempo

File name:	20190220 - Classical Strings - A Maj - 100bpm	⌄
Save as type:	Sibelius 7 (*.sib)	⌄
∧ Hide Folders		Save Cancel

Above: This is a tried-and-tested method of file-keeping.

PLAYBACK

As well as speed, composing your score in Sibelius on your computer also gives you the serious advantage of instant playback.

LISTEN TO THE MUSIC

Sibelius's Player allows you to hear the score instantaneously. You can choose to use Sibelius's default sounds or import your own and craft mixes that you think are the best representations of how the track might sound. Most of these options are found in the Play tab.

Above: The Play tab is where you can configure how your music might sound outside of the score.

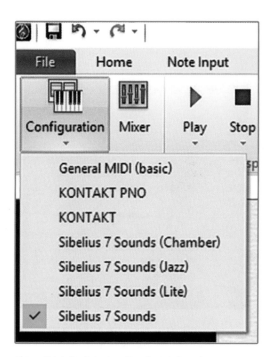

Above: This is the playback configuration window, where you can choose what samples Sibelius will utilise during playback.

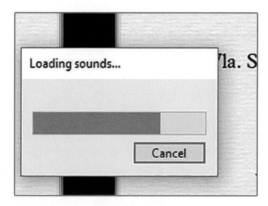

Above: It will only take a couple of minutes to have access to Sibelius Sounds once you've opened your score.

Configuration

For playback, Sibelius will make use of MIDI Sounds ('General MIDI'), or a derivation of the sounds made by the Avid Orchestra, including 'Sibelius Sounds (Chamber),' 'Sibelius Sounds (Jazz)', or 'Sibelius Sounds' – the default option.

Sibelius's sound library is large (roughly 35GB) as it consists of deeply sampled, realistic-sounding instruments with multiple velocity layers. The software will load up instruments and their attached sounds in the background, but it might take a couple of minutes before you're able to play the score. If you add new instruments and new performance techniques or expressions, these may also require another round of buffering by your system in order to play back accurately.

Hot Tip

While it's satisfying to hear your ideas back, don't become over-reliant – it's easy to write for what sounds good on Sibelius and forget about writing idiomatic parts for performers.

ADDING YOUR OWN SOUND LIBRARIES

You can load external samplers to use in Sibelius, widening the scope for high-quality sounds. Check out the advanced tips on pages 124 and 125 for information on how to do this.

AUDIO ENGINE OPTIONS

The audio engine determines how and where you produce sound from your system. Generally, you can use Primary Sound Driver, as this will link to the sound output in the settings dictated by your system, but if you have an external audio interface connected, select this through Play > Setup > Audio Engine Options > Audio Interface. From here, you can also choose your preferred sample rate and buffer size.

Right: The Setup button is located on the left-hand side of the Play tab.

Sample Rate

Sample rate is the number of samples of audio carried per second, resulting in different levels of detail in the audio recorded. For film, the industry standard is 48,000Hz, written as 48kHz, and for audio, it is 44.1kHz.

Hot Tip

If you're not getting sound out of your system, make sure the sample rate matches up with your system-wide sample rate.

Buffer Size

When recording audio, all systems need time to process the recording and its information. You can select how long it takes by adjusting the buffer size. The lowest you can go is 16 samples, with the highest being 1024. Windows users can download an ASIO driver that will

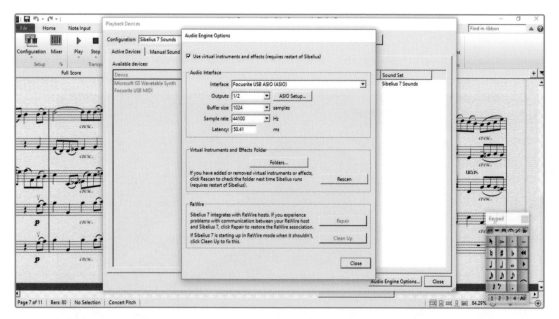

Above: This might seem complicated, but a lot of the time you can set the buffer size and forget about it. If your system starts to jitter and produce clicks and pops, just raise it. Sibelius's default will provide what's necessary for most users.

increase the maximum sample rate to 2048 samples. The higher the buffer size, the longer it will take to hear the audio, but there will be the added benefit of fewer clicks and pops, and less power being used.

THE MIXER

You can access the mixer via the keyboard shortcut M or through View > Panels > Mixer. It is laid out like a traditional recording console, consisting of a level fader for each instrument, pan pot, solo and mute buttons, group volume levels controlled by 'busses' and a master fader controlling the volume of the whole mix.

Hot Tip

If you can't see a function of the mixer, they can all be toggled into or out of view by the icons at the side, as shown in the below image.

Above: The mixer works as any audio mixer would. Craft the sound of your score here.

ADDING EFFECTS

Effects can be added to an instrument by the traditional notation conventions. You can add a delay or another effect by creating a technique and typing w/ FX with FX being replaced by the effect of your choice, including delay, chorus, flanger and more. A comprehensive list of available effects is found at Play > Interpretation > Dictionary.

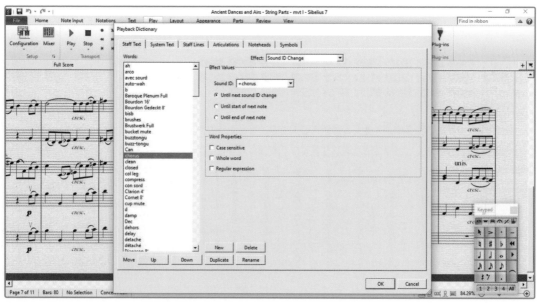

Above: Create interesting textures through the use of effects in your score.

TRANSPORT OPTIONS

Transport is found either via View > Panel > Transport or in the Play tab. Bringing the panel up will bring a control section to the forefront, allowing you to fast-forward, rewind, jump to a section, play, pause, stop and record – all of which are common features on audio playback equipment. You can also tell Sibelius to play by hitting the space bar.

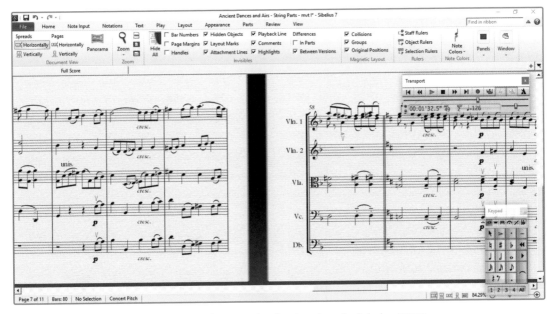

Above: The features found on the Transport panel are the same as those found on other audio playback equipment.

Hot Tip

To play from a certain section, select a note in any instrument at the beginning of the section you'd like Sibelius to play back and press P.

PERFORMANCE

Sibelius has a variety of controllable features that help produce more realistic performances of your music, giving you instant feedback on how your piece might sound.

Below: Sibelius's performance features are located in the Play tab: Live Tempo, Live Playback and Interpretation.

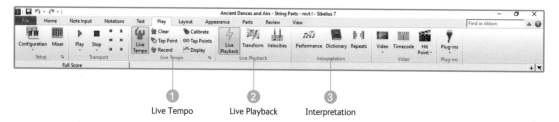

①	②	③
Live Tempo	Live Playback	Interpretation

① LIVE TEMPO

You can fine tune the tempo of your score with MIDI information, which is especially helpful for when you intend to map out tempo changes. To use this, visit Play > Live Tempo > Record and tap the tempo of your piece while it's playing. Sibelius will map this tempo – make sure to record on a lower buffer size to increase accuracy!

Above: Press this button to start measuring your tempo.

❷ LIVE PLAYBACK

Live Playback captures the nuances of live performance when played into Sibelius via a MIDI controller. If Live Playback is On (depressed and highlighted blue), expressions in your score will not be performed unless they're placed on notes inputted through the keypad. Turn it off to hear Sibelius's interpretation.

Hot Tip

When starting a score, if you're unsure of the tempo, use the Live Tempo to find it. It is also called Tap Tempo.

Velocities

Velocity means the force with which a note is played. The higher the velocity, the louder the note and vice versa. You can view and edit velocities for live playback by clicking Play > Velocities. When enabled, a vertical blue bar will appear above notes entered via MIDI. You can edit this by clicking anywhere in the blue bar; the closer to the top, the higher the velocity and vice versa.

Above: The blue velocity bar; click anywhere in the bar to change it.

③ INTERPRETATION

The Interpretation section of the Play tab is where most of the heavy lifting towards realism happens.

Performance

Add reverb, feel and metre options here to make your music feel more realistic; see the image below for suggested settings. To get the most efficient use out of this, it is necessary to have a basic knowledge of traditional Italian musical terminology. If you don't, just remember that the drop-down menu works from Less at the top to More at the bottom.

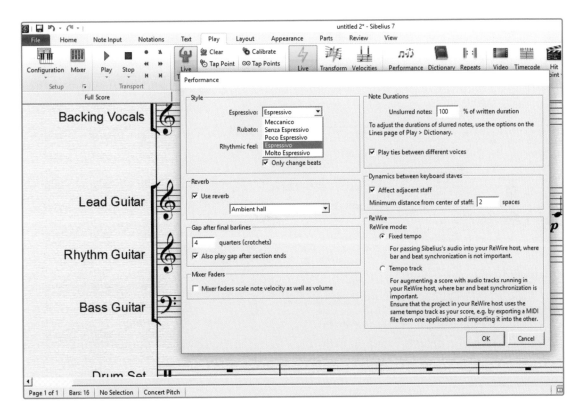

Above: Suggested settings for the Performance dialog box. These will give a basic, but natural sound, enabling you to focus on the music.

Playback Dictionary

Here, the available techniques, expressions, system and stave text and other commands are available to include as text, markings and so on. You don't usually need to edit these, but should the situation arise, it is all controlled here.

Repeats

Turn the performance of repeat sections on or off.

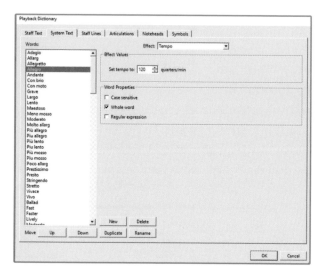

Above: If you feel that the tempo is not quite right, but don't want to add a metronome, modify it here.

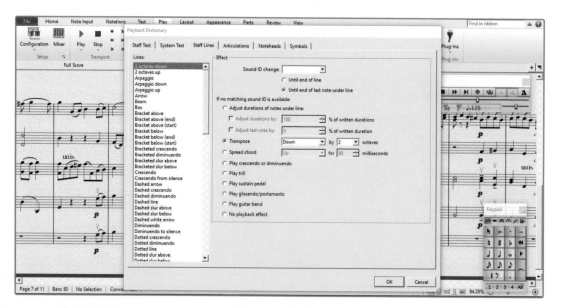

Above: The dictionary shows every command available to be used in Sibelius.

PERFORMANCE PLUGINS

As with the other sections, there's a multitude of handy plugins available to use, including Quarter Note Playback, Harmonics Playback, Ornament Playback and more, allowing you to hear the specific effects you've directed Sibelius to employ. To use these, highlight a section that involves a plugin, choose Play > Plugin and select the plugin of your choice. This will bring up a dialog box stating how notes will be changed; press OK. Once completed, Sibelius will show you how many notes have been changed.

Hot Tip

You can edit tempo text (in Stave Text) to ascribe a different metronome marking to a particular tempo text if you feel it suits your score better.

Above: On this score, no harmonics have been added. Remember to add the specific technique or expression before scanning the score.

WORKING WITH VIDEO

If you're preparing a score for a film, or perhaps preparing a scoring session to record a film's music, Sibelius's workflow and integration can make the whole process of idea to finished product seamless.

OVERVIEW

Import the video by clicking Play > Video > Import. Once imported, Sibelius will automatically synchronize the start of the video with the start of the score.

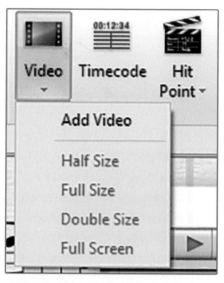

Above: Follow the instructions above to import video to your score.

Accepted Formats

Sibelius accepts many video formats, of which the most common are .avi, .mov, .mpg and .wmv (Windows Media Video).

Changing Volume and Size of the Video

You can determine the size of the video on the screen using the buttons in the bottom-left of the video dialog box. There's also a volume slider so you can simulate how loud the film's dialogue might be against the music.

TIMECODE

Timecode is the specific notation of time showing you and others working to the footage exactly

Hot Tip

If you close the video, you will need to re-open it via View > Panels > Video.

where you are. You can choose where it's placed, how often timecode is shown, whether it's on a per-bar basis, and more via Play > Video > Timecode. It is shown in Hours:Minutes:Seconds:Milliseconds.

HIT POINTS

Hit points communicate points of interest with which the music should synchronize. Create these while the footage is playing by clicking Hit Point at the desired moment. You can use this to your advantage when writing, or when giving it to a conductor and ensemble who might be recording the score.

Above: A hit point provided in the form of timecode.

EXPORTING YOUR SCORE

Similar to a Digital Audio Workstation, Sibelius can export your mix of the track, either in full or as individual instrument tracks.

OVERVIEW

Sibelius exports offline, meaning you don't have to wait the length of the score for it to finish. Rather, it is only limited by the speed of your system. Files are exported at 44kHz/16-Bit. Other sample rates and bit-depths are available, depending on your system's capabilities.

EXPORTING A FULL SCORE

When you're happy with the sound of your score, go to File > Export > Audio and you'll be presented with multiple options. If you want to export a selection of the score, place the playback marker to the point from which you'd like to export and select Export from playback line position.

Left: Export options in Sibelius.

EXPORTING INDIVIDUAL TRACKS

Export individual tracks by selecting as little as one bar of the preferred stave. Highlight multiple staves to include more.

EXPORTING MIDI

Export MIDI in the same way as Audio, but select MIDI at the export stage. The MIDI page will present you with a number of dialog boxes – there is no need to change any of the settings here: just click Export, name your track and you are finished. The exported file contains MIDI for the whole piece. You're able to load the MIDI into any DAW and the piece will exist in the same incarnation as in Sibelius.

Sibelius will warn you when a stave is selected, ensuring you're aware of what you're about to export. Make sure the tracks are labelled properly!

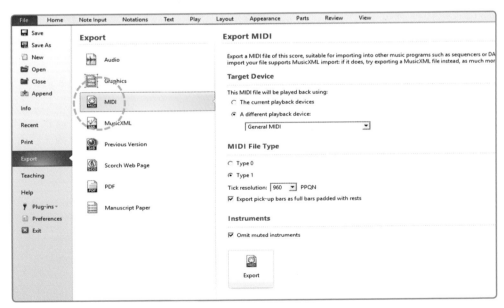

Above: Exporting MIDI allows you to bring your score into a Digital Audio Workstation, with full control over note velocity, duration and more.

SHARING YOUR SCORE

You've exported your score and it all looks pristine. You're now ready to give parts to be performed!

CREATING PARTS

Parts are created through Parts > New Part. Select which instrument(s) will go into the part and click OK. This will open a new tab in the score containing your part. Any changes made in the score will be reflected in the parts and vice versa.

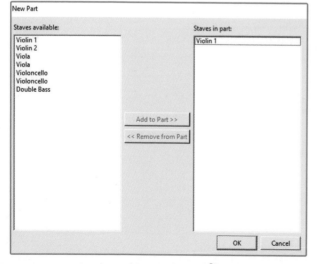

CUSTOMIZING PARTS

Once your parts are created, you might find that the layout has changed. We've already seen the best techniques to fix your layout; just repeat these to re-order anything that has gone awry. Changes made to a part will be carried over to the main score.

Left: Create your parts based on who will be reading them. You want to make it as easy to read as possible.

Number of Bars

Perhaps the main aspect of a score's visual layout to check is the number of bars per system. Eight is perhaps the maximum, but it could be lower. For about three minutes of music, try to keep the individual part down to two pages, if possible.

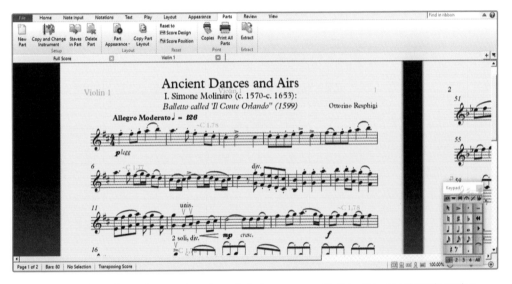

Above: Try to keep what performers have to read on a line-to-line basis as easy as possible. This might mean reducing the number of bars per system.

Hot Tip

Remember to transpose your scores to the correct keys for those who need it!

EXPORTING THE PDF OF YOUR SCORE

Exporting the PDF of your score is similar to exporting the audio. Navigate to File > Export > PDF. You can export the score and your newly created parts in one file or multiple files. To keep the PDF filename the same as the Sibelius file, don't enter anything in the Filename box.

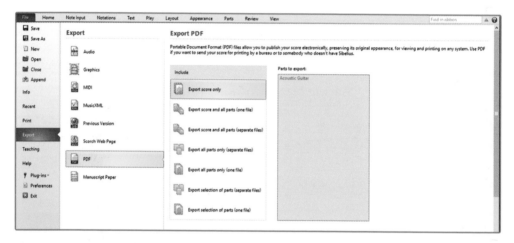

Above: The many different options for creation and exporting of parts and a full score.

PRINTING

Just like a written document, printing is as easy as saving. Select File > Print and select the appropriate options based on the print preview provided on the right-hand side of your screen.

Above: An ideal score – try to ensure your score is as easy and clear to follow as possible.

Hot Tip

Be mindful of how your score will be presented to performers; do you want them to have individual pages or use double-sided paper when performing?

GIVING AND RECEIVING FEEDBACK

You can also share your work with others to receive (hopefully!) positive feedback on it.

REVIEW AND ADDING COMMENTS

The Review tab (found at the top of the ribbon) can play host to insightful comments from your peers regarding your score. To insert a comment, click Review > New Comment. You can select Highlight first to draw attention to what you'd like to comment on. Select Comment and enter your thoughts in the dialog box. Press Esc to confirm.

Hot Tip

Comments aren't kept on the score when exported as a PDF.

Above: In the comment section, you can highlight particular sections of your score for your peers to comment upon.